Butterflies

HOW TO USE THIS BOOK

Read the captions in the eight-page booklet and, using the labels beside each sticker, choose the image that best fits in the space available.

•

Don't forget that your stickers can be stuck down and peeled off again. If you are careful, you can use your butterfly and moth stickers more than once.

•

You can also use the butterfly and moth stickers to decorate your own books, or for project work at school

LONDON, NEW YORK, MUNICH, MELBOURNE, DELHI
See our complete product line at
www.dk.com

Written and edited by David John
Designed by Polly Appleton

First American Edition, 2001
06 07 08 10 9 8

Published in the United States by DK Publishing, Inc.
375 Hudson Street, New York, New York 10014

Copyright © 2001 Dorling Kindersley Limited

All rights reserved under International and Pan-American Copyright Conventions. No part of this publication may be reproduced, stored in a retrieval system, or transmitted in any form or by any means, electronic, mechanical, photocopying, recording, or otherwise, without prior written permission of the copyright owner. Published in Great Britain by Dorling Kindersley Limited.

CIP data available from the Library of Congress

ISBN 0-7894-7867-6

Reproduced by Colourscan, Singapore
Printed and bound in China by L.Rex

Dorling Kindersley would like to thank:
Photographers Frank Greenaway, Colin Keates, Dave King, Jerry Young, Kim Taylor, Jane Burton; the Natural History Museum;
Polly Appleton, Sheila Collins, and Robin Hunter for design assistance; Kate Bradshaw, Selina Wood, Jo Rose, and Lucy Hurst for editorial assistance

See our complete product line at www.dk.com

Habitats

Butterflies and moths living in temperate climates like Europe and North America are inactive in the cold months and must hibernate. But some have learned to migrate long distances to warmer weather. Species from cold, mountain climates have darker colors, which absorb sunlight more easily. The heat of the tropics produces the most marvelously colored species. This may be for camouflage in lush vegetation, or to warn away predators.

Dappled dwelling
The Common Glider butterfly likes woodland glades. Light dappling through the trees makes its colored wing pattern difficult to spot.

Royal road runner
The rare Royal Assyrian butterfly flutters at low altitudes near roadsides in Indonesia and Malaysia.

Blue bombshell
South America has some of the most dazzling butterflies in the world. This Morphos butterfly is prized for its striking blue wings.

Black and white beauty
The striking Argent and Sable moth is found in most temperate climates of the world.

Hidden drinker
The well-camouflaged Drinker moth is common in Europe, where it lives in marshes and ditches. It sips dew from plants.

Monarch airways
The Monarch butterfly makes long-distance flights from Canada to its winter quarters in Mexico. Having survived the winter, the Monarch heads back north.

Forest recluse
Because it lives high up in the dense, steamy forests of New Guinea, very little is known about the beautiful Purple Spotted Swallowtail.

Heading for the sun
The Cloudless Sulphur migrates to areas far from its winter range in Mexico. Many fly as far as the Carribean and the southern United States.

Blue hair
The Hewitson's Blue Hairstreak butterfly lives in the tropical regions of South America.

Common and dull
The Acacia Carpenter moth is one of the most common in Australia. Its colors are dull, but it has a strong, robust body.

Cave dwellers
The Australian Bogong moths can cover the walls of buildings as they rest during migration. The moths fly south to caves in the Australian Alps, where they spend the hot, dry months.

In search of summer
The Hummingbird Hawk moth migrates from the warm southern parts of Europe to the northern parts as the spring turns to summer.

Dead animal lover
Although the Purple Emperor likes flying high up in trees, the males are attracted to the ground to feed on animal carcases.

Spectacular Swallowtail
This exotic Cattle Heart Swallowtail is common in parts of Central and South America. It can be seen flying along the edges of rain forests.

Banana lover
The Banana Eater butterfly of New Guinea loves feeding on ripe bananas.

Life Cycle

Butterflies and moths are easy to spot because of their beautiful wings and graceful fluttering. But, before they are seen as adults, butterflies and moths pass through three other life stages – egg, caterpillar, and pupa. At each stage, the insect grows and changes its form. Eventually, a butterfly or moth emerges, and flies away to feed on plants. It then lays eggs, and begins the life cycle again.

1. Two heads?
Butterflies mate end-to-end. These mating Asian Swallowtails look like a two-headed butterfly!

2. Choosing baby food
The female Cinnabar moth chooses the plant on which her caterpillar will feed. She sticks her eggs firmly to the plant with a secretion from her body.

3. Growing caterpillar
Inside this tiny egg, a caterpillar is growing. If it lives in a temperate climate, the caterpillar will stay inside its shell all winter until it is warm enough to survive outside.

4. Breaking free
Gradually, the egg darkens, and the caterpillar prepares to hatch. This one has begun to cut itself out of the egg, using its sharp jaws to create a lid.

6. Fully emerged
The new caterpillar wriggles out of the egg headfirst. It does this quickly, because it is vulnerable to predators while escaping the egg. Once free, it eats its own nutritious empty egg.

5. A bug is born
After a huge effort, the caterpillar's head emerges from the egg, and it rests for a bit. You can see the eyes on either side of its head, and also the sharp jaws it used to break through.

7. Hungry caterpillar
Caterpillars spend most of their time eating, in order to store energy for when they pupate. They use their mouth parts to chomp leaves, sometimes stripping whole plants.

EGGS, CATERPILLARS, AND PUPAS

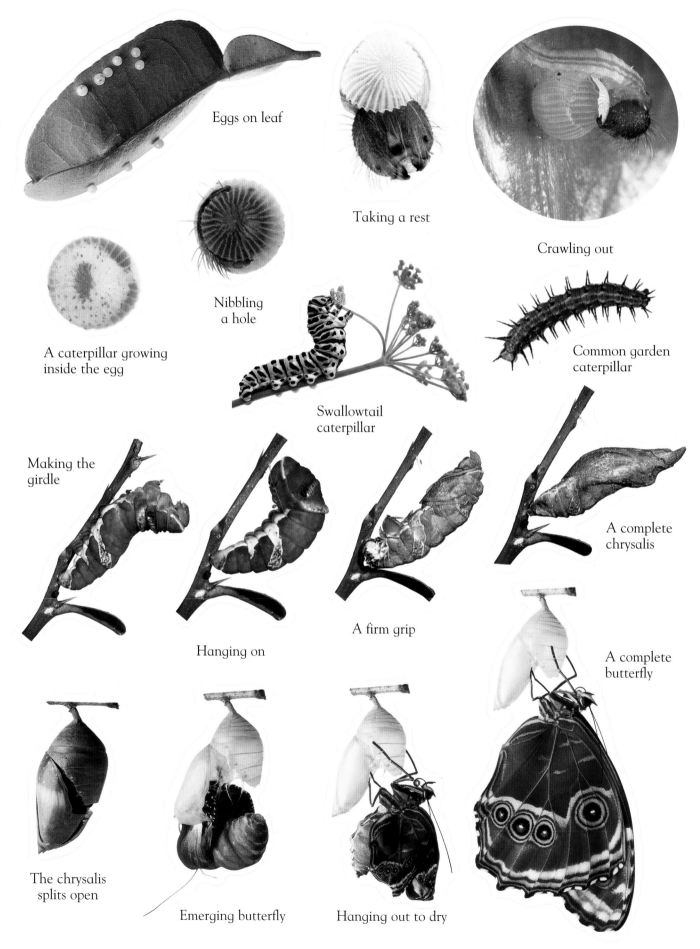

Eggs on leaf

Taking a rest

Crawling out

A caterpillar growing inside the egg

Nibbling a hole

Swallowtail caterpillar

Common garden caterpillar

Making the girdle

Hanging on

A firm grip

A complete chrysalis

A complete butterfly

The chrysalis splits open

Emerging butterfly

Hanging out to dry

COLOR & CAMOUFLAGE

Blue Hairstreak
butterfly

Cocoon leaf
camouflage

Clubtail
butterfly

Yellow
caterpillar

Green leaf
disguise

Red-banded
Pereute

Monarch
butterfly

Zebra caterpillar

Banana Eater

Indian Leaf
butterfly

Smooth Emerald

The Wizard

Purple
Emperor

Owl eyes
on wings

Common Glider

Yellow
Drinker moth

Morphos
butterfly

Midilid
moth

BRIGHT & BEAUTIFUL

Birdwing Swallowtail

Zebra Swallowtail

Cloudless Sulphur

Adonis Blue

Cattle Heart Swallowtail

Napoleon Dynastor

Mating Asian Swallowtails

Purple Spotted Swallowtail

Corsican Swallowtail

Coppery Dysphania

Orange Albatross

Royal Assyrian

Queen Alexandra's Birdwing

Large Copper

MOTHS

Luna moth

Cinnabar moth
laying eggs

Sloan Uraniid
moth

Hummingbird Hawk

Chalcosiine moth

Hornet Clearwing

Zodiac moth

Argent and Sable moth

Pericopine moth

Madagascan
Moon moth

Millar's Tiger moth

Acacia
Carpenter
moth

Saturniid moth

Australian
Bogong moth

9. Strap in
Next, the caterpillar spins a loop of silk, like a safety belt, that it sticks to the stem and passes around the middle of its body for support.

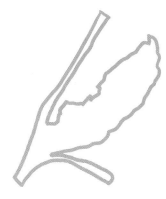

10. Coming out
Slowly, the caterpillar's skin splits along the back and a pupa begins to emerge.

8. Getting ready
This Citrus Swallowtail is preparing to form its pupa. First, it selects a plant stem and spins a silken pad. It then sticks its tail to the pad.

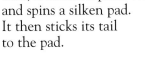

11. Hidden magic
The pupa is complete, and a wonderful metamorphosis is taking place inside.

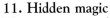

12. Berry disguise
This pupa looks like an unripe berry.

13. Getting changed
Before it emerges, the color of a new butterfly becomes visible in the pupa.

15. Born again
Once outside, the butterfly has a rest and pumps blood into its crumpled, new wings.

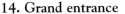

14. Grand entrance
The pupa splits, and the new insect struggles out into the world.

16. New identity
The butterfly expands its wings rapidly before they harden, and its beautiful new identity is revealed.

Survival in a hostile world

In order to conceal themselves from predatory birds, caterpillars, butterflies, and moths find ways of protecting themselves. Some "disappear" into their surroundings by resembling bark or dead leafs. Others display warning colors, which suggest they are poisonous or distasteful to eat. And some species have wings patterned with spots that resemble large, fierce eyes – something that would startle most birds!

Tastes bad
Birds sense that this Chalcosiine moth is nasty to eat, because of its lurid warning colors.

Dead leaf defence
Little is known about the small Midilid moth, but it seems to have a very effective decaying leaf camouflage.

Indian leaf-trick
Can you spot this Indian Leaf butterfly sitting on a twig? It avoids birds by brilliantly "disappearing" into its surroundings.

Don't eat me!
Caterpillars can be hairy, poisonous, camouflaged, or have sharp bristles, like this prickly creature. Anything to keep the birds away!

Leafy hideaway
Butterflies and moths choose where to lay their eggs very carefully. Under a leaf is often a good hiding place. Only a few of the eggs laid will survive long enough to hatch. The rest will be eaten by predators.

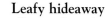

Poison eater
The Sloan's Uraniid moth has a taste for poison. As a caterpillar, it feeds off plants that are poisonous to most other creatures, which makes it distasteful to predators.

Red decoy
The bright red spots on
this Clubtail butterfly's wings distract
predators from attacking its body.

Playing dead
The dead leaf
appearance of
this moth cocoon
helps to conceal
it in the wild.

Laid-back flyer
This Pericopine moth
is often found in great
numbers. Its bold pattern
and slow, daytime flying
suggest that predators
think it tastes nasty.

Giving you the eye
When this Saturniid moth
moves its upper wings, it
reveals "eyes" that scare
off enemies.

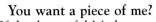

You want a piece of me?
If this beautiful Madagascan
Moon moth is attacked by a
predator, its long, trailing hind
wings will come off, giving the
moth a chance to escape.

Eye see
This fierce-looking
butterfly frightens its
enemies by displaying a
large "eye" on its wing.
It looks more like a
hunting owl than a
delicate insect!

There's no crossing this zebra
The Zebra caterpillar has poisonous,
spiky horns to keep its predators away.

Wasp or moth
The Hornet Clearwing moth looks
like a nasty hornet and even flies
like one. Few predators would be rash
enough to risk attacking a hornet!

Endangered species

Butterflies and moths are dependant on wild plants and open countryside. This make them vulnerable to changes in the environment, especially those caused by humans. In recent times, many beautiful species have become rare, then endangered, then extinct. People's need for land and agriculture threatens their habitats, and deforestation reduces their numbers and variety.

Grazers wanted
In Europe, the lovely Adonis Blue is threatened because its grassland habitat is no longer grazed by rabbits or sheep.

Beautiful Birdwing
One of the largest known butterflies, the Queen Alexandra's Birdwing, is now very rare because it is hunted by collectors and its forest habitat is being destroyed.

Urban casualty
Although the Zebra Swallowtail can still be found in North America, it is threatened by the destruction of its food plant, and by urban growth.

Down the drain
The beautiful Large Copper butterfly is now extinct in Britain. Land drainage caused the loss of its marshy habitats.

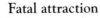

Fatal attraction
The Luna moths of North America are decreasing in number due to insecticides and urbanization. The moths are attracted to street lights making them vulnerable to predators.

Rain forest mystery
The large Dynastor Napoleon butterfly is so rare that very little is known about it. It flies only at dusk in Brazilian rain forests, where deforestation threatens its habitat.

Collectors will be prosecuted
The Corsican Swallowtail is found only in the mountains of Corsica and Sardinia. Collecting them is now forbidden by law.